■SCHOLAST

Partner Poems

for Building *Fluency*

40 Engaging Poems for Two Voices With Motivating Activities
That Help Students Improve Their Fluency and Comprehension

Timothy V. Rasinski • David L. Harrison • Gay Fawcett

New York • Toronto • London • Auckland • Sydney
Mexico City • New Delhi • Hong Kong • Buenos Aires   **Teaching** *Resources*

Cover design by Maria Lilja

Interior design by Sarah Morrow

Illustrations by Teresa Anderko, Maxie Chambliss, James Graham Hale, Anne Kennedy, and Mike Moran

Copyright © 2009 by Timothy V. Rasinski, David L. Harrison, and Gay Fawcett

All rights reserved. Published by Scholastic Inc.

Printed in the U.S.A.

ISBN-13: 978-0-545-10876-8

ISBN−10: 0-545-10876-4

5 6 7 8 9 10   40   16 15 14 13 12

Contents

Introduction

Reading fluency is the ability to read accurately, quickly, effortlessly, and with appropriate expression and meaning (Rasinski, 2003).

DLH:

In this book, we'll explore why poetry is such a useful tool for helping emerging readers develop fluency. We'll focus on poems for two or more voices. I hope you like the poems because I'm your poet. I wrote most of the pieces especially for this book. A few have appeared in previous collections.

We all have favorite stories that illustrate what we want to say. Here are two of mine that illuminate the connection between poetry and fluency. The first occurred in Kuala Lumpur, Malaysia.

A thin little girl stood beside me, facing the class. The weight of all those expectant eyes was nearly more than her fragile frame could bear. Her gaze clung desperately to the paper in her hand, her poem. When she began at last, her whispery voice barely reached students in the first row.

I had a friend with a wild snake—

Her brother played with the snake that nearly bit him—

My friend and I panicked and called for an ambulance—

It arrived five minutes later—

Her brother suddenly woke up—

Their mother came home and got cross with us—

But still I thought it was funny—

"Good work!" I assured the young poet as she melted onto her chair with relief. We were writing memory-based poems and my exquisitely shy young friend had presented us with a humorous one.

Sadly, most of the class missed the whole thing. I wanted the poet to read her poem again with more gusto. I ached for her to read it like she wrote it and must have felt it, but I was afraid she might die of fright right there in front of us.

My glance fell on another girl, one who had been the life of the party all week. Nothing shy about that one! Inspiration struck.

"I think this poem might be even more fun if it were told in two voices," I suggested to the poet. "How about adding sound effects? Would you like to work with a partner and read for us again tomorrow?"

Blessedly, Life of the Party's hand shot up. The poet smiled her relief. So did I. The deal was sealed.

The girls huddled in the back of the room. Before long I heard giggling. By the next day the reticent poet seemed more confident and her friend could scarcely sit still until their turn came. I had no idea what was coming. Their performance went like this:

(POET)	(LIFE OF THE PARTY)
I had a friend with a wild snake—	
	Hissssssssssssss
Her brother played with the snake that nearly bit him—	
	Owwwwwwww
My friend and I panicked and called for an ambulance—	
	Ring ring
It arrived five minutes later—	
	Ee-ow ee-ow
Her brother suddenly woke up—	
	Yawn
Their mother came home and got cross with us—	
	Whoops!
But still I thought it was funny—	
	Ha ha ha!

This time the class got it. Appreciative laughter at all the right places did wonders for the poet. I don't mean that she suddenly blossomed into a drama queen or a perfect reader, but the experience gave her a much needed shot of confidence. I think she learned that day that reading aloud does not have to be terrifying.

In this case, turning the poem into a reading for two voices made all the difference. Knowing she had a partner gave the shy girl courage. She read her poem without the hesitation and uncertainty that had haunted her the previous day. Working together, the girls delighted in ferreting out opportunities to turn the poem into a mini-production. They not only got the big picture, they were successful in communicating that picture to the class.

Here is my second example. A six-year-old girl in Missouri was given a picture book in which a dog interviews everything he discovers in his master's garden. The girl listened while her mother read in the dog's voice and in the other voices. The girl read the book to herself, first silently then aloud. She asked an adult friend to join her and they took turns reading.

The following morning the girl took the book to school and organized her classmates into teams. As the two-voice episodes were read aloud she coached her friends to act out the roles of the characters. The words in the storybook were still the author's, but the joy of discovery belonged to the children.

Fluent readers get inside the words and make them their own. Fluency breathes life into flat symbols on a page so that they leap into multidimensional characters complete with mental pictures, sounds, songs, rhythms, smells, and even dance steps.

Poems can stimulate fluency because their messages tend to be simple and kids can relate to what they read. For many young readers, poetry seems personal, like a note from the poet just for them. Good poetry for young people rings true. Subjects are consistent with their experiences, hopes, fears, and dreams. The humor is their humor; they get the jokes. If a poem makes them sad, they cry for the right reasons and understand what moved them.

The thrust of our book is about the role that multivoice poems can play in the process of improving reading fluency. If, along the way, you and your students find yourselves writing poems of your own, I promise that they will be as much fun to write as they are to read.

TVR:

I am a firm believer in the teaching of basic reading skills or competencies: children are most likely to be successful in learning to read when they are provided with top-notch instruction in phonics (word decoding), vocabulary (word meaning), reading fluency, and comprehension. I also continue to see myself as a whole-language teacher. I believe that children learn to be literate and can learn basic reading skills through authentic and engaging experiences with real literature.

With the publication of the report of the National Reading Panel (2000) and subsequent enactment of Reading First, there has been a proliferation of programs and approaches for teaching the basic reading skills in ways that I find less than authentic. I see children being taught phonics by sounding out nonsense words. I see children learning vocabulary by mindlessly writing and memorizing definitions to words that have little connection to their own lives. I see children learning fluency by being encouraged to read faster and faster, charting their reading speeds on graphs, always trying to improve on the previous day's reading rate. And I see children being assessed for reading comprehension by teachers who simply count the number of words that students provide in the retelling of a passage. All of these activities and others like them may improve student performance in these areas and lead to improvements on progress-monitoring tests. But I sincerely wonder what kind of impact these sorts of activities will have on students' love of reading, their desire to read, and the purpose they see for reading. We may be developing a generation of children who can go through the motions of reading but who see little intrinsic value in or purpose for doing so. This is one of my worst educational nightmares.

When award-winning poet David Harrison approached me about the opportunity to use his original poetry as a starting point for enjoying poetry and for teaching the basic and essential skills for reading, I jumped at the chance. I enlisted the help of one of my best friends and professional colleagues, Gay Fawcett, to help flesh out the project.

The result of our three-way collaborative effort is this book of poetry and reading instruction. At the heart of the book are David's delightful poems for two voices. These poems have intrinsic literary value that will help children learn to love poetry and the language of the poet. Moreover, because they are poems for two voices, they require children to work together to make the poems come alive for a listening audience. Yet, the poems can stand alone as literary art.

There are 40 poems, more than enough if you wish to introduce a new poem each week. How you use this book is up to you, but I'll make a suggestion. I love the idea of working with one poem per week, devoting five to ten minutes per day to the week's selection. Early in the week introduce students to the poem. Read it aloud in as expressive and meaningful a manner as possible. Talk about the poem and what it means and what emotions it evokes. Then read it again, and have students read it chorally with you several times and in different ways. As the week goes on, give students more responsibility for the poem. Have them read it with various partners and incorporate some of the fluency activities described on pages 9–13. By midweek, have students work with you on the comprehension activity for each poem. On the last day of the week have pairs of students perform the poem for the class or another audience (parents visiting the classroom, school principal, other classes). Because students know they will be performing the poem for an audience, they will have a natural reason for practicing (repeated readings) the poem. Moreover, the focus of their practice will be on reading with expression and meaning (the real fluency), not mere reading speed.

Over the course of the year, as students master more and more of the poems from this book, they can select their own poems from previous weeks to read and perform at an end-of-the-week poetry slam. Through a routine such as this one, students will develop essential skills necessary for becoming proficient readers. They will also develop a wonderful affection for reading, for poetry, for oral reading performance, and for language that will last the rest of their lives.

Published research is beginning to show that poetry can have a powerful impact on students' literacy development. Rasinski and Stevenson (2005), for example, report that at-risk readers who were given the opportunity to read simple rhymes with their parents on a regular basis made significantly greater gains in word recognition and fluency than students who had the same instruction in school but without the opportunity to read poetry with their parents. Lori Wilfong's (2008) Poetry Academy program in a public school resulted in positive gains in elementary students' word recognition, fluency, comprehension, and confidence in reading. Moreover, in both studies the students (and adults) reported thoroughly enjoying the opportunity to practice and perform poetry!

However you choose to use this book, our most important advice is to enjoy the poems and activities—and help your students to see the enjoyment possible in such activities. Best wishes, and—as they say in the business—break a leg!

GF:

Children and poetry—it's a natural! Step onto any playground in the country and you will quickly be surrounded by young children and poetry. You'll hear "Mabel, Mabel, set the table" from the jump-rope girls on the blacktop. You'll hear "I see London, I see France, I see Joey's underpants" from the rowdies on the jungle gym. You'll hear "Lily and Brandon sitting in a tree, k-i-s-s-i-n-g" from the teasers. When the bell rings, follow them into the classroom and notice how the teacher has their total attention when she pulls Shel Silverstein from the shelf.

Yet, as they get a little older, many students profess to disliking poetry. Follow them home, however, and you'll see that's a lie. Listen as they sing the lyrics of their favorite pop songs. Watch as they dance to the rap on their iPods. Ask them to repeat the jingles of television commercials. Regardless of the age group, children are naturally drawn to poetry—especially when it connects to their lives or makes them laugh like the partner poems in this book will do.

Poetry and fluency—that's just as natural a pairing as children and poetry! The cadence and rhyme of poetry beg for a fluent reading. The brevity of most poetry lends itself to fluency practice. The visual structure of poetry serves to remind readers of phrasing and expression.

The partner poems in this book are fun just as they are, but if you have students who could benefit from some fluency instruction (and who doesn't?), there are a number of instructional strategies you can use with any poem in this book. What follows are specific strategies that research has shown to be effective in building fluency and, subsequently, comprehension.

Strategies for Using Partner Poems to Enhance Fluency

Model Fluent Reading

In order for students to understand that fluency and good reading are more than just fast reading, they need to hear what fluent reading sounds like. In this way, they come to understand that good, fluent reading involves making meaning with one's voice during reading. Perhaps the best person to provide that model is the teacher (or parent, if this book is being used at home). We encourage teachers to partner up with fellow teachers (or the principal, or another adult), select a favorite two-voice poem from this book, rehearse, and then perform the poem for students. Teachers can also partner with students. Be sure that when you practice, you work on reading with appropriate expression and volume. Work on emphasizing certain words and phrases. Experiment with raising and lowering your voice at different places in the poem. When you are confident that you can read it fluently with your partner, then it's time to "take the show on the road!"

Perform your poem for your own class of students and, if possible, share it with other audiences: other classes during "poetry breaks"; the entire school during morning announcements; in the cafeteria during lunchtime; for parents at the beginning of a PTA or other parent meeting.

Be sure that after you perform your poem, you talk with students about how you used your voice to make meaning. Explain that you practiced your poem by yourself and with your partner several times, and that you experimented with different ways to read the poem to convey just the right message to your audience. If you read the poem to a friend or colleague as a trial run to get some feedback, tell students about that too. By talking with students, you will help them understand that fluency means reading with expression and meaning, and that the most important way to learn to read fluently is to practice the poem several times and get feedback and help from others. Students will learn that they have to go through the same process when they prepare their own poems for reading.

Repeated Reading

Repeated reading is a fluency strategy that's been well established in the research literature (Rasinski & Hoffman, 2003; Samuels, 1979) and endorsed by the National Reading Panel (2000). Repeated reading simply refers to practicing a passage several times until it can be read with appropriate expression and meaning. The research has shown that when students engage in repeated reading, they improve in word recognition, fluency, and comprehension, not only on the passage that they practice but on new passages not previously read (Rasinski & Hoffman, 2003; Rasinski, Padak, Linek, & Sturtevant, 1994; Samuels, 1979; Stahl & Heubach, 2005).

The problem you may face when implementing repeated reading with older students is motivating them to read a poem multiple times. A solution to that dilemma is to tie the repeated reading to a performance; most students are willing to practice in order to shine when performing.

You may simply wish to call repeated reading "rehearsal," because that is what it essentially is—practicing a passage so that it can be read to and appreciated by an audience. Implementing repeated reading with the partner poems in this book is simple, yet research shows it can yield great results for your students. Simply ask your students to read a poem several times until they achieve a level of fluency. Be sure the repeated reading or rehearsal is not aimed at reading the poem fast (as is often the case in some fluency programs) but to read the poem expressively and meaningfully and with sufficient volume and confidence (stage presence) that an audience will enjoy the reading.

One idea to make our partner poems work in your classroom is to assign a different partner poem to several pairs or groups of students. The pairs could practice together for several days (there's the repeated reading) in preparation for a poetry slam on a Friday afternoon. Students should not be required to memorize the poem for the performance, but simply be prepared to read it aloud. They can perform for their own classmates, for another class, or even for parents or community members. In the following weeks, rotate the poems to different pairs or groups of students.

Choral Reading

Assisted reading (Rasinski, 2003) is a fluency strategy that involves a less fluent reader reading a text while simultaneously listening to a fluent rendering of the same passage by someone else. Choral reading (Rasinski, 2003) is an assisted-reading fluency strategy that involves groups of readers reading a text together. Students who are less fluent benefit from hearing a more fluent reading of the passage while reading it themselves. The process of reading and hearing the passage read simultaneously leads to improved reading. In addition to improving reading, choral reading is a superb way to develop the sense of teamwork and common purpose that we all strive for in our classrooms.

Poetry is ideal for choral reading as poems can easily be performed by a group. Our partner poems offer unique possibilities for choral reading. Instead of having individual students read each partner's part, have groups of students chorally read the parts of each partner. In order for groups to read in unison and with appropriate expression, plenty of practice (repeated readings) will have to be done.

Paired Reading

Paired reading (Rasinski, 2003) is another assisted-reading fluency strategy that involves two readers reading a passage together. When one of the readers is not as fluent as the other, the less fluent reader benefits from hearing the passage read while reading it himself or herself. The process of hearing it read fluently while reading it aloud will lead to significant improvements for both partners.

Our partner poems, again, are ideal for paired reading, as the poems themselves are made for two readers. As partners begin rehearsal they can engage in paired reading, reading both parts together. As rehearsal continues, they can choose their own parts for individual practice and eventual performance. When paired reading is integrated into the rehearsal process, students will benefit from both the paired reading and the repeated readings that are part of rehearsal.

Recorded Reading

A recorded reading of a poem can be used both as an opportunity for assisted reading practice or as a type of performance that can motivate rehearsal. To use a text for assisted reading, you simply need to record a fluent reading of a partner poem. This could be a recording of you reading a poem with a partner, which is a nice outcome for the poems that you modeled live for your students with a fellow teacher (see Model Fluent Reading on page 9), or it could be a fluent recording done by some of your students who have rehearsed the text. The recording can be in the form of an audiotape that becomes part of a library of recorded readings or as a podcast that is stored on a computer. Then, your students who are working on a poem can listen to the fluent recording while reading it themselves. After a bit of practice with the recorded version they should be able to read the poem on their own.

Once students have rehearsed a poem to the point where they can read it with fluency, you can offer to record their reading of the poem. This recording can be a form of performance that will be a strong incentive for students to engage in rehearsal (repeated readings). Once the recording is made, it can be added to the library of recordings in your classroom, sent to a library in another classroom, or even sent home so that parents can listen to their child's poetry performance. The possibilities for using audio recordings in developing fluency and performing partner poetry are nearly endless.

Read It Like the Character

Prosody is that aspect of fluency that involves reading with expression. To be able to read with appropriate expression and phrasing (even when reading silently) requires readers to have some degree of understanding of what they have read. In many programs for teaching fluency, prosody is often sacrificed for speed. We think that prosody is essential for fluent reading and good comprehension. We feel also that poetry lends itself well to reading with prosody, and our partner poems, because they are written in the voices of children and involve a conversational dialogue between partner readers, are particularly well suited for developing prosody.

One way for students to notice and develop prosody in their reading is to engage in a fluency activity we call Read It Like the Character. Simply put, we want students to become the characters that David has developed in his partner poems. As your students listen to others read these partner poems, ask them if they are able to hear the voices of the characters who are supposed to be speaking in the poems. Talk with your students about how they view the characters from the poems. How would they describe the characters? What sort of mood are they in? Are the characters frightened, cranky, rambunctious, sleepy, silly, energetic, or what? What in the poem or in the reading of the poem by others makes students describe the characters in this way?

Then, when students begin to rehearse the poems on their own, ask them to try to read as the character they have described. You may wish to model this many times on your own and to coach your students in how they may make their voices capture the characters they wish to portray.

Another way to extend this activity is to describe a character prior to reading a partner poem, or have students describe a character they would like to create. Then, when students rehearse a partner poem, they need to try to put that character into the reading of the poem—to read it like the character. When a poem is then performed for the class, students can discuss the character that the reader tried to create in the performance. It is amazing to see how students are able to create characters and meanings with their voices and just a little rehearsal.

Lucky Listener

Lucky Listener is a performance strategy that motivates students to read and reread a poem multiple times (repeated readings). Once students have rehearsed and performed a poem, you don't want students to put the poem away, not to be seen again. If a little bit of practice in rehearsing the poems is good, more practice in performing the poems is even better.

A Lucky Listener is simply another person (or animal) who may be lucky enough to hear the performance of a student's poem. Once students have mastered a poem and performed it for the class, ask them to find others to listen to them read their poem. This can be other students or teachers in school, or parents, siblings, other family members (including pets), and neighbors. The Lucky Listener listens to a reader read a poem (with the partner poem, it could be the entire poem, with all parts read by one student) and then on the reverse side of the written poem (or on a Lucky Listener form; see page 15) signs his or her name along with a comment about what he or she liked about the poem and the reading. If mom listens to her son read a poem twice in one evening she signs the back side of the poem or form twice and can make two comments on the reading. If dad hears his daughter read her poem three times (twice as soon as he comes home from work and once before she goes to bed), he signs the poem or form three times and adds three comments. If Grandma listens to her grandson read over the phone, the student can write in Grandma's name in the appropriate place. Although dogs and cats cannot sign their names, they may identify themselves with a paw print on the Lucky Listener sheet.

Students return to school the next morning and compare Lucky Listener sheets. Whoever has the most signatures can be designated the Lucky Listener Champ for that day. Many students will come to school with ten to twenty signatures on their sheets. They have a ball reading for someone and receiving deserved praise for their reading. What they often do not realize is just how much they are improving their reading skills with such practice.

Harvesting Words

Fluency involves learning to recognize words effortlessly (automatically) as well as accurately. Our partner poems in this book contain wonderful words that can expand students' word recognition skills and vocabulary. We call it harvesting words.

Here's how it works. Once students have had a chance to practice a poem, ask them to notice any interesting words in the poem. We usually ask students to choose anywhere from one to six words for each poem. Then you ask students to call out or harvest their choices. The words are written on a classroom chart for easy visual access. You can also have students write them in their personal word journals.

We recently watched Ms. Crawford, a second-grade teacher, lead her class in several choral readings of the poem "Brussels Sprouts." After reading and talking about how the students did, Ms. Crawford asked her students to harvest some words, which she quickly wrote on a blank sheet of chart paper hanging on the wall. The students chose these words: *Brussels, sprouts, cottage, cheese,* and *pickled.* Ms. Crawford herself added *cauliflower* because she said she had just prepared it for her family's dinner the night before. After writing each word she gave a quick explanation of it and asked students to provide any additional information they knew about it. Then, throughout that day and the next, she encouraged students to use the words in their own conversations. To encourage students to do so, she took the lead in finding ways to use the words. She referred to her youngsters as young sprouts, hoped that their minds were not pickled, and she threatened to give them Brussels sprouts and cauliflower if they didn't behave themselves. The students picked up on her having fun with words and began to use them in their own speech throughout the days. Most of the words we adults add to our own vocabularies are done in much the same process—noticing a new word, determining its meaning, and then using the word in our own personal language.

Strategies for Using Partner Poems to Enhance Comprehension

While poetry offers a natural opportunity to develop reading fluency, it is all for naught if students do not comprehend what they are reading. The activities you will find for each partner poem in this book are designed to increase reading comprehension by inviting students to think about the meaning of each poem.

Reading comprehension is the process of using prior experiences and the author's text to construct meaning that is useful to that reader for a specific purpose (Irwin, 1991). In order to comprehend, readers are actively engaged in many meaning-making activities, including: (1) activating prior knowledge, (2) examining the text to determine the length, structure, and important parts, (3) making predictions, (4) determining big ideas, (5) making connections to their own experiences, (6) creating mental images, (7) monitoring their understanding, (8) generating summaries, and (9) evaluating texts (Tompkins, 2007).

For each poem, the comprehension activity features an instructional strategy designed to develop one or two comprehension skills. However, it is important to keep in mind that the comprehension process is recursive, that is, the skills are not isolated when one is reading. Rather, the reader flows in and out of predicting, visualizing, questioning, and so on throughout the entire text. Although you may find one comprehension strategy specifically connected to a partner poem, we encourage you to think about how the strategy can be applied to other poems and, especially, about how more than one comprehension skill is at work simultaneously while the student reads. In order to help the student become metacognitively aware of his or her comprehension, the activity directions explain how the activity will help him or her become a good reader.

The activities we describe in this section can be done one at a time or in combination with one another. We hope you will try them out with your students and find just the right mix to meet their needs. There is no magic formula for becoming a good, lifelong reader. The key is to read a lot and to engage in activities that get students to think deeply about what they have read and how they have read, and at the same time to have an enjoyable experience. We think that our partner poems can go a very long way to help you help your students develop a lifelong love of reading, a deep affection for poetry, and significantly improve their fluency, comprehension, and overall reading skills.

> *These poems were written for fourth to sixth graders. Please preview them and decide if they are appropriate for your students.*

Lucky Listener

Read your poem aloud to someone—a family member, friend, neighbor—anyone can be a Lucky Listener! Once that person listens to you read the poem, ask him or her to sign below and indicate what he or she liked about the poem and how you read it. If the listener listens more than once, he or she can sign the form multiple times. Even your pets can listen to you read (think of ways that they can sign their name!). Try to collect at least five signatures.

Name of Student: _____

Name of Poem: _____

Lucky Listener's Name	Date and Time of Reading	Comments on the Poem and the Reading

Baby Talk

(ADMIRER)

Awww,
iddn't him coot?

Wook at dat
tweet widdle nose.

Him jus' tweet
enough to eat!

He reminds me
of Unca' Frank.

He almost looks
like him could talk.

(BABY)

**They don't think
I understand
a word they say.
I'm not "coot,"
I'm cold.
My diaper's wet.**

**Oh please.
Give me a break.**

**Whoa, back off.
You're scaring me!**

**The guy
with the ball cap?
I don't think so!**

**Lady, if you
only knew.**

Baby Talk

Comprehension Activity: Reading for Meaning

Directions: Good readers show that they understand what they're reading when they read with expression. Find a partner and read "Baby Talk." One partner will read the part of the baby and the other partner will read the part of the admirer. Read it the way you think the characters would really say those lines. After you've practiced several times, join with two other partner teams. Each team will take a turn reading the poem. Vote for the best performance.

Best Baby Talker

Award for Best Performance

of "Baby Talk"

Brussels Sprouts

(CHILD)

What are those
green things?

I don't want no
Brussels sprouts.

I don't want no
Brussels sprouts!

I don't want no
Brussels sprouts!

If I taste these
Brussels sprouts,
then can I have
something else?

Ugh!
I hate these
Brussels sprouts!

Please pass the
Brussels sprouts.
I don't want no
chicken liver.

(PARENT)

Brussels sprouts.

**Any.
Come on, try some
Brussels sprouts.**

**Any.
These are special
Brussels sprouts.**

**Any.
Just one taste of
Brussels sprouts.**

Sure!

**Here's some yummy cottage cheese,
pickled beets, cauliflower,
lima beans, and chicken liver.**

Any.

© 2009 *Partner Poems for Building Fluency* Scholastic Professional

Brussels Sprouts

Comprehension Activity: Discussion Web

Directions: Good readers *form opinions* about the message of the text by *drawing on their own experiences.* Work with a partner to complete the discussion web below. Generate as many reasons as you can for both the "yes" box and the "no" box. Then draw a conclusion based on your reasons and record it in the box below.

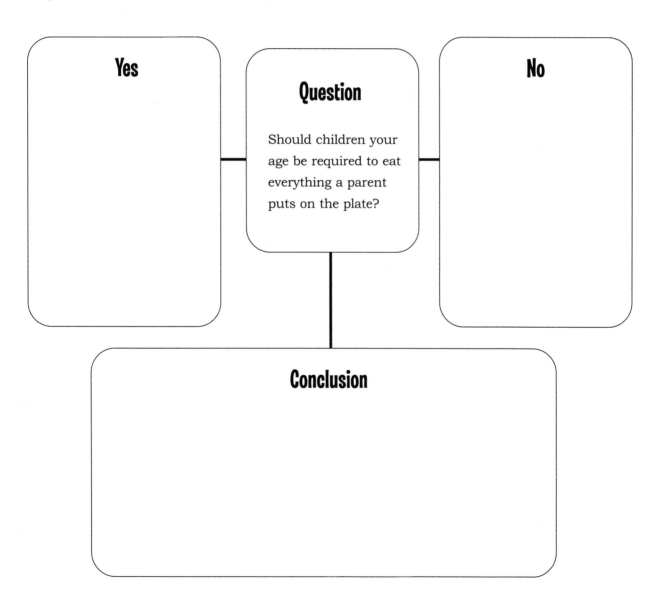

Yes

Question

Should children your age be required to eat everything a parent puts on the plate?

No

Conclusion

Now, on your own, write a paragraph supporting your conclusion. Find a new partner and read your paragraphs to one another. Discuss what was the same or different about your conclusions.

Cleaning Your Room

(MOTHER)

Did you put
your games away?

(CHILD)

Yes, Mother.

Did you pick up
all your books?

Yes, Mother.

Fish tank?

Yes.

Hamster?

Yes.

Pick up all
your dirty clothes?

Yes, Mother.

Make the bed?

No.

You have a reason,
I suppose?

**I'd have to move my games
and books and tank and cage
and dirty clothes.**

Cleaning Your Room

Comprehension Activity: Sketch to Stretch

Directions: Good readers visualize as they read. *Visualizing* is when you picture in your mind the events of a story. Visualizing helps you better interpret the text and notice things you might have missed before. Listen as two people in your class read the partner poem "Cleaning Your Room." Visualize what is happening in the poem. Sketch a picture of what you've visualized. Don't worry about your artwork. The goal is to get your ideas down without words.

Describe your sketches. Compare them to those of your classmates. How were your visualizations alike? Different?

He Poked Me!

(SISTER)

He poked me!

Did too.

Too.

Too.

What?

Ha ha ha.

Did not.

Not.

Not.

What?

He started it.

Did too.

Too.

Too.

Yours.

Yours.

This is boring.

Let's go somewhere else to play.

(MOTHER)

Stop!

Poking her.

Stop what?

Stop!

You're making me crazy!

Screeeeeeam!

Shreeeeeek!

(BROTHER)

Did not.

Not.

Not.

What?

Make her stop.

She laughed at me.

Did too.

Too.

Too.

What?

Did not.

Not.

Not.

Your fault.

Yours.

Yours.

I agree.

He Poked Me!

Comprehension Activity: Connecting With the Text

Directions: Good readers make sense of what they are reading in one of three ways: (1) Sometimes they get information directly from the text by simply *reading the lines*. (2) Sometimes the author gives hints but the reader has to figure the meaning out by *reading between the lines*. (3) Sometimes the reader forms opinions by connecting to his or her experiences even though the text does not give any clues. That is *reading beyond the lines*.

You know by <u>reading the lines</u> that the children are poking one another and laughing at each other. Now read between the lines. How do you think the children feel about each other? Why do you think so?

_____

_____

_____

_____

Read <u>beyond the lines</u>. What do you think will happen next? Why do you think that will happen?

_____

_____

_____

_____

Just One More Store

(CHILD)   **(MAMA)**

I just sigh
When Mama says . . .

                    Just one more store.

My legs hurt.
My toes are sore.
My feet are growing
To the floor.

                    Just one more store.

She never stops
To drink or go.
How she does it
I don't know.

                    Just one more store.

She holds it up
And puts it down
In every store
All over town.

                    Just one more store.

I've never been
So bored before.
How I hate
This awful chore
With Mama pulling
Toward the door . . .

                    Just one more store.

Just One More Store

Comprehension Activity: Making Inferences

Directions: Sometimes writers state information directly in the text; other times, readers must infer information from details in the text. Decide whether the following statements are true or false, and then think about how you knew. Did the poet say so in the poem, or did you use a detail from the poem to infer?

The mother in the poem loves to shop.   True or False

How do you know? _____

The child's toes are sore.   True or False

How do you know? _____

The child's legs hurt from walking so much.   True or False

How do you know? _____

The child is bored.   True or False

How do you know? _____

The child has been standing in one spot too long.   True or False

How do you know? _____

The mother should have hired a babysitter.   True or False

How do you know? _____

Write your own stanza to add to the poem. Reread the whole poem to a friend.

Use the back of this sheet or a separate piece of paper.

Not My Turn

(DOG)	(PARENT)	(1ST CHILD)	(2ND CHILD)

Woof, whine,
whimper, whimper.

**Someone
let the dog out.**

Not my turn.

Is too.

Bark, howl,
scratch, scratch.

**Someone
let that dog out!**

Oooooooo!

**Someone
get the paper towels!**

Not my turn.

Is too.

Not My Turn

Comprehension Activity: Making Connections

Directions: Good readers *use their own experiences* to make sense of the text. Use the form below to take two-column notes that help you make connections between the partner poem and your own experiences.

List three actions that took place in the poem.	Write what each action made you think about from your own experience.

What do the poem and your connections make you think about?

_____

_____

_____

_____

Owa Dagoo Siam

(BIG BROTHER)   **(LITTLE BROTHER)**

Big bros
Help little guys
So say these words
Until you're wise:
Owa
Dagoo
Siam.

                                    Owa
                                    Dagoo
                                    Siam.

Say them faster
Little man.

                                    Owa
                                    Dagoo
                                    Siam.

Faster faster
If you can.

                                    Owa
                                    Dagoo
                                    Siam.

Say them till
You understand!

                                    OwaDagooSiam!

Oops!

I think I'd better go.

                                    Imagaw
                                    Nagetchu
                                    Bro!

Owa Dagoo Siam

(Oh, what a goose I am!)

Comprehension Activity: Making Inferences

Directions: Sometimes writers state information directly in the text; other times, readers must infer information from details in the text. What can you infer about the big and little brothers? List some words to describe each.

Words that describe the big brother	Words that describe the little brother

Write about their relationship.

_____

_____

_____

_____

We Don't Wanna!

(CHORUS)   **(KIDS BEGGING)**

We don't wanna
We don't wanna
We don't wanna
We don't wanna

We don't wanna	We don't wanna
We don't wanna	Go to bed, we
We don't wanna	Wanna read a
We don't wanna	Book instead.
We don't wanna	We would rather
We don't wanna	Play with toys.
We don't wanna	We won't make a
We don't wanna	Single noise.
We don't wanna	All our friends stay
We don't wanna	Up till ten; we'll
We don't wanna	Never never
We don't wanna	Ask again.
We don't wanna	We don't wanna
We don't wanna	Go to bed; we
Let's stay up all	Wanna play all
Night instead!	Night instead!

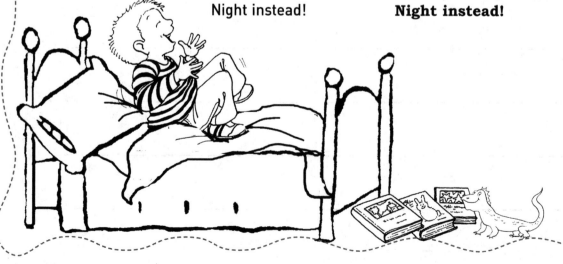

© 2009 *Partner Poems for Building Fluency* Scholastic Professional

We Don't Wanna!

Comprehension Activity: Making Personal Connections

Directions: Good readers *use their own experiences* to make sense of the text. Brainstorm a list of things you would prefer to do rather than go to bed.

I don't wanna go to bed. I wanna . . .

Write a new stanza for the poem.

_____

_____

_____

_____

Practice reading the poem with your new stanza, then read it to your classmates.

Two O'Clock in the Morning

(1ST VOICE)	(2ND VOICE)	(3RD VOICE)
Drip		
Drop		
Drip		
Drop		
	Waah!	
		Make that
		water stop!
Pleep		
Pleep		
Pleep		
Pleep		
	Argh!	
		I can't get
		to sleep!
Plunk		
Plink		
Plunk		
Plink		
	Stop	
		that dripping
		in the sink!
	I can't	
	stand it!	
		I can't sleep!
Drip		
Drop		
Pleep		
Pleep		

© 2009 *Partner Poems for Building Fluency*   Scholastic Professional

Two O'Clock in the Morning

Comprehension Activity: Problem-Solution Mapping

Directions: Good readers can *identify problems and solutions* in the texts they read. Identify the problem in the poem "Two O'Clock in the Morning." Think of three possible solutions to the problem and what the outcome would be for each solution.

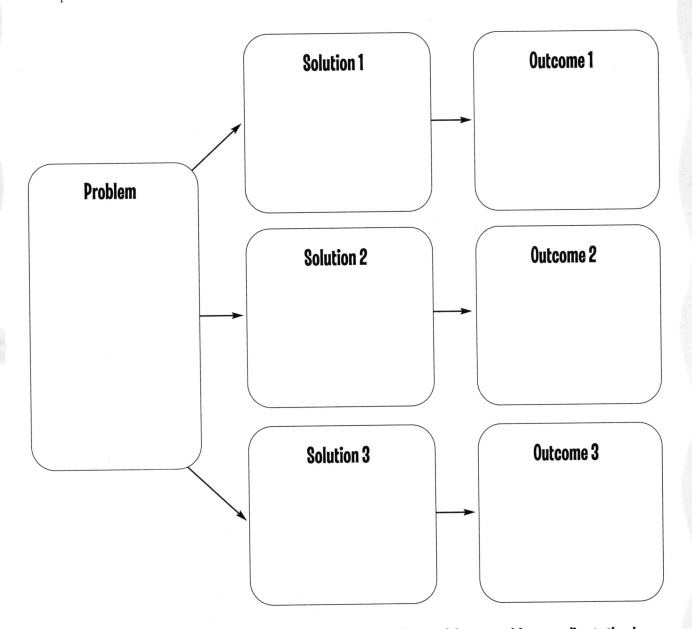

Choose one of your solutions and write an ending to the poem. Then read the poem with your ending to the class.

You may write on the back of this sheet or on another piece of paper.

Waking Up Sis

(BIG SIS)

Good morning, Sweetie!

Time to rise and shine.

Get up now or you'll be late.

Don't make me have
to ask again.

Don't you pull that
stuff on me.

Okay, now I'm getting mad.

I'll break your legs
and feed you to the dog!

Time to rise and shine,
Sweetie!

(LITTLE SIS)

snore

snore

snore

snore

snore

snore

Whut?

**Okay.
Thanks,
I'm on it.**

© 2009 *Partner Poems for Building Fluency* Scholastic Professional

Waking Up Sis

Comprehension Activity: Somebody Wanted But So (SWBS)

Directions: Good readers recognize the *elements of a plot*. Complete the chart below to show the plot elements in "Waking Up Sis."

Somebody (characters)	Wanted (goal)	But (conflict)	So (resolution)

Using the Somebody Wanted But So chart, map out a time when you didn't want to get out of bed. Write a paragraph about it.

Use the back of this sheet or a separate piece of paper.

The Grump!

(1ST VOICE)	(2ND VOICE)
Perfect day!	
	I think not
Warm weather	
	Sticky hot
Smell the flowers	
	Makes me sneeze
Pet a kitty	
	No, I'll wheeze
Feed some birdies	
	Hate their litter
Pat a bunny	
	Nasty critter
Gentle clouds	
	Feels like rain
You're so gloomy	
	You're a pain
So much joy	
	So much rot
I think positive	
	I think not!

The Grump!

Comprehension Activity: Making Connections

Directions: Good readers make sense of what they read by *making connections* to information and events they have experienced, observed, or read about. Are you more like the grump or the optimist? Make a deeper connection to the poem by writing your own poem or paragraph about a "perfect" day from the perspective of a grump or an optimist. (You may use the back if you need more room.) Read your poem aloud to a partner.

Brainstorm words, phrases, and images for your poem :

My Perfect Day

When Furniture Talks

(NARRATOR)   **(TABLE)**   **(CHAIR)**   **(BED)**

Said the table
To the chair,

**"Life's not easy,
Life's not fair.
She loads me down
With useless clutter,"**

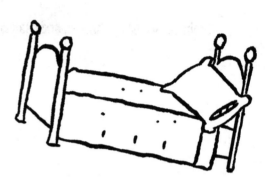

Said the table
With a mutter.
Said the chair
To the table,

*"I'd gladly trade
If I were able.
He plops his bottom
On my lap
Until I think
My legs will snap."*

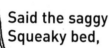

Said the saggy
Squeaky bed,

***"Be grateful you're
Not me instead.
All night long
They toss and snore.
I need sleep.
My back is sore."***

Every word
Of this is true.
Furniture
Has feelings too!

© 2009 *Partner Poems for Building Fluency* Scholastic Professional

When Furniture Talks

Comprehension Activity: Personification

Directions: Good readers think about what might happen next. Imagine what each piece of furniture would say or write in its diary if the people who lived in the house went on a two-week vacation and the house was empty. You will be personifying the furniture. Personification is when an author gives human characteristics to nonhuman objects.

Table

Chair

Bed

Ants at a Picnic

(1ST VOICE)	(2ND VOICE)	(3RD VOICE)	(4TH VOICE)
Humans playing volleyball!			
	Where there's volleyball there's food!		
		On the table!	
			Lunch is served!
Man, man! Fried chicken!			
			Beans! Beans! The magical fruit!
	Oh! Wow! Lemonade!		
		Ooo, I love potato salad!	
			Help! I've fallen in the dip!
Someone pass the cheese, please.			
		Yuck! A fly fell in the gravy!	
	Whoa! I saw that cookie first!		
What a picnic!			
	What a day!		
		Uh-oh! Run!	
			They've got spray!

Ants at a Picnic

Comprehension Activity: Visualizing

Directions: Good readers make pictures in their heads as they read. *Visualizing* is when you picture in your mind the events of a story. Visualizing helps you better interpret the text and notice things you might have missed before. Visualize a scene from the poem and sketch it. Be ready to share your picture with your classmates.

Cows

(1ST VOICE)	(2ND VOICE)	(3RD VOICE)	(4TH VOICE)
Farmer calls us so we go			
	Swaying gently to and fro		
		Walking easy, mooing low	
			Moving toward the barn we go
Moving toward the barn we go			
	Walking easy, mooing low		
		Swaying gently to and fro	
			Plodding patiently we go
Plodding patiently we go			
	Swaying gently to and fro		
		Walking easy, mooing low	
			Chewing on our cud we go
Chewing on our cud we go			
	Walking easy, mooing low		
		Swaying gently to and fro	
			Farmer calls us So we go
So we go	**So we go**	*So we go*	***So we go***

© 2009 *Partner Poems for Building Fluency* Scholastic Professional

Cows

Comprehension Activity: Vocabulary and Visualizing

Directions: Good writers use strong words in their work. Strong words help you visualize or picture in your mind the events of a story. Visualizing helps you better interpret the text and notice things you might have missed before. The poet uses strong verbs in this poem to help you visualize what is happening. Choose a different animal and write your own version of the poem. Use the Brainstorm Box to come up with some strong verbs you could use, and write your poem in the space below the box. You may use the back if you need more room.

Animal chosen: _____

Brainstorm verbs:

Poem:

Gir-Mouse

(FATHER GIRAFFE)

I'm glad I am
your hubby, Dear.

(MOTHER MOUSE)

I'm glad I am your wife
even though you're just
a teensy tall.

Yes I am, my dearest one,
while you, I must admit,
are rather small.

Our daughter is
a lovely girl!

I wouldn't change a thing,
except that squeak she gets
from you, I suppose.

What about her
six-foot neck?

What about her
pointy little nose?

I love those knobs
between her ears.

I love her twitchy tail.
Having a gir-mouse girl
is so much fun.

Our gir-mouse girl
is a beautiful thing!

I can't wait to have
a gir-mouse son!

Gir-Mouse

Comprehension Activity: Sketch to Stretch

Directions: Good readers visualize as they read. *Visualizing* is when you picture in your mind the events of a story. Visualizing helps you better interpret the text and notice things you might have missed before. Listen as two people in your class read the partner poem "Gir-Mouse." Visualize what is happening in the poem. Sketch a picture of what you've visualized. Don't worry about your artwork.

Create your own animal combination and give it a name.

Use the back of this sheet or a separate piece of paper. Share your sketch with your classmates. Ask them to interpret your sketch before you describe what you have drawn.

It's So Cold

(1ST VOICE)

It's so cold this winter
I told a joke that turned to ice.

A robin's tongue
froze to a worm.

But the worm won't go.

(2ND VOICE)

**We had to thaw it
by the fire
to see if it
was funny.**

**We boiled them loose
and the robin flew,**

**Claims he wants
to stay till days
turn sunny.**

It's So Warm

(1ST VOICE)

It's so warm this winter
our furnace is in therapy.

Squirrels are playing
In the sprinkler.

It's so warm
that millipedes
are wearing shorts.

(2ND VOICE)

**I saw a snowman
thumbing
a ride north.**

**Our house
peeled down
to its
undercoat!**

 Told with Ryan Brinkerhoff. © 2009 *Partner Poems for Building Fluency* Scholastic Professional

It's So Cold • It's So Warm

Comprehension Activity: Figurative Language

Directions: Hyperbole is a technique used by authors or speakers when they exaggerate to make a point. The poems "It's So Cold" and "It's So Warm" grew out of a "whopper" contest David Harrison had with a young friend. Trying to outdo a partner by making up outrageous stories (whoppers) that couldn't possibly be true is an enjoyable battle of wits. Use hyperbole to describe a weather condition (such as a rainstorm, snowstorm, hurricane, etc.). Find a partner and have a "whopper" contest of your own, trying to outdo each other's description of weather conditions.

My weather condition: _____

_____

_____

Hyperboles:

Last Three Leaves

(1ST LEAF)	**(2ND LEAF)**	**(3RD LEAF)**
Look at them down there		
	Piling up against fences	
		Swirling around hikers' shoes.
Think it hurts to fall that far?		
	No, silly, leaves don't hurt.	
		Good, because I'm losing my grip.
So am I!		
	Ditto!	
		Ready?
On the next breeze		
	We'll meet on that heap	
		Where kids are leaping.
I'll miss this tree		
	But look what	
		Lies ahead!
One . . .		
	Two . . .	
		Three!
Wheeeee!	**Wheeeee!**	*Wheeeee!*

Last Three Leaves

Comprehension Activity: Making Predictions

Directions: Good readers *predict* what will happen next in the story. What do you think will happen next to the leaves? Imagine what the leaves will say once they have landed after falling from the tree, and what the tree might say to the leaves. Compare your predictions to your classmates' predictions. Are they different but still logical?

What the leaves might say after they have fallen:

What the tree might say to the leaves:

Write your own poem.

On the back of this sheet or on a separate piece of paper, write a poem about what the leaves might say after they've fallen. Read your poem aloud to a partner.

Truckaderms

(1ST READER)	(2ND READER)
Nose to tail they lumber down the highway	
	Grazing on gray miles, following the herd past one more exit,
One more hill,	
	Until late under silent sky
They seek rest side by side	
	With others of their kind.

Truckaderms

Comprehension Activity: Vocabulary and Visualizing

Directions: Good writers use strong words in their work. Strong words help you visualize or picture in your mind the events of a story. Good readers visualize as they read. *Visualizing* is when you picture in your mind the events of a story. Visualizing helps you better interpret the text and notice things you might have missed before.

How did the verbs in this poem help you visualize what is happening?

_____

_____

_____

Choose a stanza and sketch the image you visualize for that part of the poem.

Groanosaur Test

(TEACHER)

What do you call
a dinosaur in a hurry?

What do you call
a dinosaur in a snowstorm?

What do you call
a dinosaur at a funeral?

What do you call
a dinosaur who likes spicy food?

What do you call
a dinosaur stuck in tar?

What do you call
a dinosaur digging a hole?

What do you call
a dinosaur pulling a wagon?

What do you call
a dinosaur who takes this test?

(CLASS)

A dino-scurry.

A dino-flurry.

A dino-bury.

A dino-curry.

A dino-tarry.

A dino-quarry.

A dino-lorry.

A dino-sorry!

(Terry Bond, who loves puns, wrote half of this poem.—DLH)

Groanosaur Test

Comprehension Activity: Sketch to Stretch

Directions: Good readers visualize as they read. *Visualizing* is when you picture in your mind the events of a story. Visualizing helps you better interpret the text and notice things you might have missed before. Listen as two people in your class read the partner poem "Groanosaur Test" and visualize the dinosaur described in each stanza. Sketch a picture of what you visualized for one of the riddles. Don't worry about your artwork. The goal is to get your ideas down without words.

Write your own question for this test and see if your classmates can get the right answer.

_____

_____

Gym Class

(1ST VOICE)	(2ND VOICE)
What's that odor?	
	Something rot?
Gag! Yuck!	
	Ugg!
What?	
	Muddy water?
Pigs?	
	Skunk?
Fish?	
	Cabbage?
Worms?	
	Gunk?
Sour milk?	
	Garbage stew?
Worse than that!	
	Oh phew!
It's fouler than a litter box.	
	Save us!
It's our gym socks!	It's our gym socks!

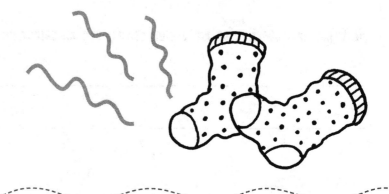

Gym Class

Comprehension Activity: Sensory Association

Directions: Some words help us make connections by associating images with one or more of our senses of sight, smell, taste, hearing, or touch. Some examples are *yummy, ouch, bam, skunky, smooth, blast*. Make a list of at least five such words or phrases and explain what they make you think of. Then, write a sentence that uses each word.

1. _____

_____

_____

2. _____

_____

_____

3. _____

_____

_____

4. _____

_____

_____

5. _____

_____

_____

Practicing

(1ST VOICE)

How will you say
you lost your homework?

That's been done
a million times.

Cats don't eat your
homework, dummy!

Boy, you better do
better than that!

Boring, boring, boring, boring!

Okay! Better!
That's more like it!

Yes! You're ready!
Now let's go to class.

(2ND VOICE)

My dog ate it.

My cat ate it?

My sister ate it!

Daddy started a fire with it.
Brother flushed it down the john.
Mama wrapped the garbage in it.

My parrot papered its cage with it.
Someone robbed our house and stole it.
I gave it to a needy child.
I accidentally wrote it in French.

Harvard wanted to see it first.
The White House made it top secret.
Aliens beamed it up to read.
It's coming out in a movie soon.
I died but I'm feeling better now.

© 2009 *Partner Poems for Building Fluency*   Scholastic Professional

Practicing

Comprehension Activity: Making Predictions

Directions: Good readers *predict* what will happen next in the story or poem. What do you think
will happen next? Write a poem or story to tell what will happen when the students go to class.
Be ready to share your piece with your classmates.

_____

_____

_____

_____

_____

_____

_____

_____

_____

_____

_____

_____

Onomatopoeia Chorus

(1ST VOICE)	(2ND VOICE)	(3RD VOICE)	(4TH VOICE)
Crash			
Bam	**Bam**	*Bam*	***Bam***
	Pow		
Wham	**Wham**	*Wham*	***Wham***
		Smash	
Bang	**Bang**	*Bang*	***Bang***
			Boom
Clang	**Clang**	*Clang*	***Clang***
Crunch			
Snap	**Snap**	*Snap*	***Snap***
	Gouge		
Tap	**Tap**	*Tap*	***Tap***
		Grind	
Bump	**Bump**	*Bump*	***Bump***
			Mangle
Thump	**Thump**	*Thump*	***Thump***
Cluck			
Growl	**Growl**	*Growl*	***Growl***
	Hiss		
Howl	**Howl**	*Howl*	***Howl***
		Tweet	
Purr	**Purr**	*Purr*	***Purr***
			Ssss
Grrr	**Grrr**	*Grrr*	***Grrr***
Sizzle			
Pop	**Pop**	*Pop*	***Pop***
	Bubble		
Plop	**Plop**	*Plop*	***Plop***
		Fizz	
Clatter	**Clatter**	*Clatter*	***Clatter***
			Rattle
Splatter	**Splatter**	*Splatter*	***Splatter***
Gulp			
Burp	**Burp**	*Burp*	***Burp***
	Belch		
Urp	**Urp**	*Urp*	***Urp***
		Giggle	
Roar	**Roar**	*Roar*	***Roar***
			Hiccup
Snore	**Snore**	*Snore*	***Snore***

Onomatopoeia Chorus

Comprehension Activity: Making Inferences

Directions: Good readers are also *good writers*. Read the poem together as a class. Use the sound clues to make up a story to go with this poem. When your teacher says "Begin," start your story and keep adding details until he or she says, "Stop." Then change seats with someone. Read the story on that desk and pick up where it left off. Keep writing until your teacher again says, "Stop." Change seats once more, read the story in front of you, and continue adding to it. Repeat this process, moving to different desks and adding to whatever story you come to, until your teacher finally says to finish the story where you're sitting.

_____

_____

_____

_____

_____

_____

_____

_____

_____

_____

Playground Conversations

(1ST VOICE)	(2ND VOICE)

Johnny's got a girlfriend!

          I'm warning you!

Johnny's got a girlfriend!

          I'm warning you!

Johnny's got a . . . OUCH!

(3RD VOICE)	(4TH VOICE)

*What did you put
for Number 1?*

          Bird

*What did you put
for Number 2?*

          Nest

*I don't need to hear the rest.
I think I flunked another test!*

(5TH VOICE)	(6TH VOICE)

Come on over after school.

          I'm grounded.

You were grounded last week too.

          I know.

How did you make your folks so mad?

          Fed my little sis a frog.

I'd be grounded forever, man!

          I am.

(7TH VOICE)	(8TH VOICE)

Johnny loves you!

          No he don't!

Johnny loves you!

          No he don't!

*Don't you know
the word is* doesn't*?*

          ***Doesn't matter—
Johnny don't!***

© 2009 *Partner Poems for Building Fluency* Scholastic Professional

Playground Conversations

Comprehension Activity: Making Connections

Directions: Good readers make sense of what they read by *making connections* to information and events they have experienced, observed, or read about. Listen to the playground conversations at your school today and then write about what you heard.

Playground Conversations at _____ **School**

_____

_____

_____

_____

_____

_____

_____

_____

_____

_____

Recess In

(BOYS)	(GIRLS)

No swinging on the swings today,
No tag, no teeter-totter,

        No sliding board, no monkey bars—
        The playground's full of water.

We're having recess in today,
It's raining like the dickens,

        The weatherman ruined our day—
        We're cooped in here like chickens.

No running after girls outside,
No chasing boys either,

        Recess out is fun and games—
        Recess in is neither!

No sliding board, no monkey bars,
No tag, no teeter-totter,

        We're having recess in today—
        The playground's full of water.

Recess In

Comprehension Activity: Vocabulary and Visualizing

Directions: Good writers use strong words in their work. Strong words help you visualize or picture in your mind the events of a story. Good readers visualize as they read. *Visualizing* is when you picture in your mind the events of a story. Visualizing helps you better interpret the text and notice things you might have missed before.

Read the poem again and list all the nouns that helped you visualize this poem.

Brainstorm some nouns about indoor recess.

Write a poem or draw a picture of indoor recess.

Use the back of this sheet or a separate piece of paper.

School Bell

(1ST VOICE)	(2ND VOICE)	(3RD VOICE)	(4TH VOICE)

What if
The school bell went off early?
What if
They let us all go home?

What if
They didn't know they did it?
What if
We left them here alone?

What if
They said, "Hey wait a minute!"
What if
They said, "You left too soon!"

What if
We laughed,
"The bell rang early."
What if
We said, "We left at noon!

What if
The school bell went off late?
What if
They kept us here till 10?

What if
They did it all on purpose?
What if
They left and locked us in?

What if
The school bell rang on time?
What if
We left and caught the bus?

What if
We made this whole
thing up?
What if
We're being silly us?

School Bell

Comprehension Activity: Cause and Effect

Directions: Good readers understand when one event causes another. Play with the idea of "what if?" Make a cause-and-effect chart by asking "what if?" and then coming up with answers. Try to think of things that would make your reader laugh. An example is in the table to get you started.

CAUSE	EFFECT
What if all vegetables quit growing?	We'd have to eat ice cream for dinner every day.

Create a poem from your list and read it to a partner.

Use the back of this sheet or a separate piece of paper.

The Library

(1ST VOICE)	(2ND VOICE)	(3RD VOICE)	(4TH VOICE)
Shhh			
	Shhh		
		Shhh	
			Shhh
Shhh!	**Shhh!**	*Shhh!*	***Shhh!***
Tiptoe in			
	Tiptoe out		
		Mustn't chatter	
			Mustn't shout
Shhh!	**Shhh!**	*Shhh!*	***Shhh!***
Find a corner			
	Find a nook		
		Find a seat	
			Find a book
Shhh!	**Shhh!**	*Shhh!*	***Shhh!***
Nowhere else			
	We'd rather be		
		Bring your book	
			And read with me.
Shhh!			
	Shhh!		
		Shhh!	
			Shhh!
Shhh!	**Shhh!**	*Shhh!*	***Shhh!***

The Library

Comprehension Activity: Compare and Contrast

Directions: Good readers can *compare and contrast* information in the text with situations in their own lives. Make a list of places where people keep their voices soft. Make a list of places where people are often loud.

Quiet Places	Loud Places

Do you prefer quiet or loud places? Why?

_____

_____

_____

The Zit

(STUDENT)   **(REST OF THE CLASS)**

I've got a zit!
An awful zit!
It's redder than
A cherry pit!

It's bigger than
A catcher's mitt!

When I found it
I admit
I screamed and yelled
And threw a fit.

He's so mad
That he could spit.

I told my parents,
"I'm unfit
To go to school
And so I quit!"

It's redder than
A cherry pit!

"I'm staying home
And here I'll sit!"

It's bigger than
A catcher's mitt!

But they said,
"Quite the opposite,
It's just a teeny
Tiny zit.

And soon you'll
Rid yourself of it."

It's just a little
Bitty bit.
We can't even
See your zit!

The Zit

Comprehension Activity: Hyperbole

Directions: Sometimes writers use hyperbole (exaggeration) to create tall tales, make a point, or add humor. Brainstorm a list of other situations that lend themselves to hyperbole. Here are some ideas to get you started: upset stomach, sore back, little sister/brother, coldest day, biggest sneeze. Choose one situation from your list, and take turns with a classmate making up exaggerated statements.

Brainstorm Box

Using Hyperbole _____

_____

_____

_____

_____

The Man in the Moon

(NARRATOR)   **(THE MAN IN THE MOON)**

The man in the moon
Eats nothing but cheese.

                    There's nothing but cheese to eat.

Often he cries
To the cheddar skies,

                    "I'm dying for some little treat!"

He dreams of chicken salad, he says,
On slices of fresh whole wheat.

                    I yearn for yams,
                    Sugar-cured hams,
                    Or anything gooey or sweet!

The man in the moon
Eats nothing but cheese—

                    There's nothing but cheese to eat—

But oh how he wishes
For tastier dishes,

                    Like salads!
                    And veggies!
                    And meat!

This poem first appeared in *Using the Power of Poetry to Teach Language Arts, Social Studies Math, and More* by David L. Harrison and Kathy Holderith (Scholastic, 2003).

The Man in the Moon

Comprehension Activity: Pourquoi Tales

Directions: Pourquoi tales are old legends or fictional stories told to explain why certain events happened. These tales often start in the past, such as "A long, long time ago..." and end when the explanation is complete. At one time, people believed the moon was made out of cheese. Try your hand at writing a pourquoi tale to explain this belief.

_____

_____

_____

_____

_____

_____

_____

_____

_____

_____

_____

Grandpa Says

(GRANDCHILD)   **(FRIEND)**

Grandpa says
When he was small
They had no TV.

                                    None?
                                    At all?
                                    No TV?
                                    What a shame!
                                    He must have had
                                    A computer game.

They didn't have
Computers yet.
Grandpa's pretty old.

                                    I bet!
                                    So what did kids
                                    In the old days do?

Grandpa says
They read.

Oooooo!   Oooooo!

Grandpa Says

Comprehension Activity: Compare and Contrast—Venn Diagram

Directions: Good readers can *compare and contrast* information in the text with situations in their own lives. Compare and contrast yourself with your grandpa or another older adult you know.

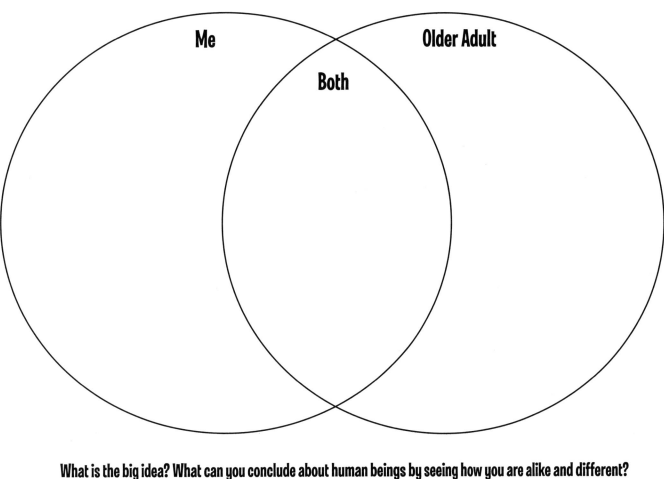

Me

Older Adult

Both

What is the big idea? What can you conclude about human beings by seeing how you are alike and different?

_____

_____

_____

_____

It's a Lollity Popity Day

(1ST VOICE)

It's a lollity popity day

It's a lollity popity
hide-and-go-seekity
read a good bookity day.

It's a lollity popity
hide-and-go-seekity
read a good bookity
roll in the grassity
talk with a friendity day.

It's a lollity popity
hide-and-go-seekity
read a good bookity
roll in the grassity
talk with a friendity
sit on a lapity
play with your petity day.

Hooray!

(2ND VOICE)

It's a lollity popity
hide-and-go-seekity day.

It's a lollity popity
hide-and-go-seekity
read a good bookity
roll in the grassity day.

It's a lollity popity
hide-and-go-seekity
read a good bookity
roll in the grassity
talk with a friendity
sit on a lapity day.

It's a lollity popity
hide-and-go-seekity
read a good bookity
roll in the grassity
talk with a friendity
sit on a lapity
play with your petity
happy-go-luckity day.

Hooray!

It's a Lollity Popity Day

Comprehension Activity: Copy Change

Directions: Copy change is a way of writing a poem by using the format of another author's poem and changing the words to make a new poem of your own. Change the words in the Lollity Popity poem to make your own poem about how you would like to spend your day. Be ready to share your poem with your classmates.

_____

_____

_____

_____

_____

_____

_____

_____

_____

_____

_____

I Love You

(1ST VOICE)	(2ND VOICE)
I love you.	
	I love you too.
I love you three.	
	I love you four.
I love you lots.	
	I love you more.
I love you first.	
	I love you longer.
I love you louder!!!	
	I love you STRONGER!
I do because I said it first.	
	I do because I said it last.
I do because I said it s-l-o-w.	
	I do because Isaiditfast.
I love you more than One hundred thousand Million billion Bags of sweets.	
	I love you more than Two jillion trillion Zillion quadrillion Chocolate treats.
I love you everything Under the sun.	
	I love you everything, Plus one.
I love you more Than I can measure.	
	And I love you, My truelove treasure.

I Love You

Comprehension Activity: Figurative Language

Directions: Good readers make meaning of the text because they *understand figurative language* the author uses. Hyperbole is when you exaggerate to make a point and what you say is nearly impossible. David Harrison was using hyperbole when he wrote,

> *I love you more than*
> *One hundred thousand*
> *Million billion*
> *Sacks of sweets.*

Find other examples of hyperbole in the poem:

Think of someone or something you love. Use hyperbole to tell how much you love them or it. Write at least five examples.

1.

2.

3.

4.

5.

My Dog, My Boy

(BOY)

I taught my dog
A funny trick.
I taught him how
To fetch a stick.

I taught him how
To sit and stay,
I taught him how
To romp and play.

I taught my dog
To take a nap
Snuggled down
Upon my lap.

(DOG)

I taught my boy
A funny trick.
I taught him how
To throw a stick.

I taught him how
To sit and stay,
I taught him how
To romp and play.

I taught my boy
To take a nap
With me snuggled
On his lap.

My Dog, My Boy

Comprehension Activity: Point of View

Directions: Good readers understand the author's *point of view.* When an author tells a story from the first-person point of view, a character in the story is talking. When an author tells a story from the third-person point of view, the story is being told by someone who is not in the story.

What point of view did the author use in this poem?

_____

_____

Who is telling the story?

(*Hint: There can be more than one speaker.*)

_____

_____

Rewrite the story in your own words using the third person point of view.

(*Hint: You will use the words* dog *and* boy *instead of the word* I.)

_____

_____

_____

_____

_____

Friends

(1ST FRIEND)

You're my friend.

If I have chocolate,
I'll give you half.

I'll blow on your hurt
If you should fall.

If you feel goofy,
I'm goofy with you.

If you're scared,
I'll share your fears.

I love it that we
Never fight (almost).

We'll be friends
Our whole lives through.

(2ND FRIEND)

You make me laugh.

**If I have spinach,
I'll give you all!**

**If you feel crummy,
I'll feel crummy too.**

**If you cry,
I'll dry your tears.**

**I love it when
You spend the night.**

**There's nothing I
Won't do for you.**

**We'll be friends
Our whole lives through.**

Friends

Comprehension Activity: Compare and Contrast—Venn Diagram

Directions: Good readers can compare and contrast information in the text with situations in their own lives. Compare and contrast yourself with your best friend.

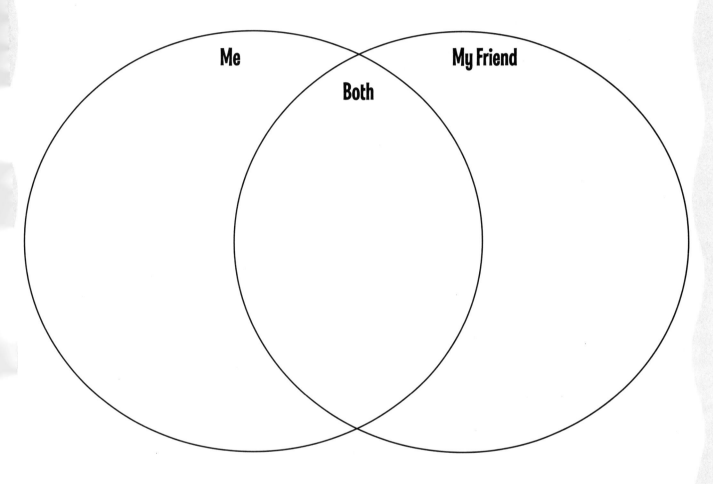

What can you conclude about friendship from your comparison?

_____

_____

_____

_____

Dinner

(BUG)	(SPIDER)	(LIZARD)

I'm a little buggy-wug,
Buggy-wug,
Buggy-wug,
I'm a little buggy-wug,
Flowers are my dinner.

I'm a little spider-ider,
Spider-ider,
Spider-ider,
I'm a little spider-ider,
Buggies are my dinner.

I'm a little lizard-izard,
Lizard-izard,
Lizard-izard,
I'm a little lizard-izard,
Spiders are my dinner.

Spider-ider won't get me,
Won't get me,
Won't get me,
Spider-ider won't get me
To be his little dinner.

Lizard-izard won't get me,
Won't get me,
Won't get me,
Lizard-izard won't get me
To be his little dinner.

The buggy flew!
The spider hid!
And now

We're
Growing
Thinner!

We're
Growing
Thinner!

We're
Growing
Thinner!

Dinner

Comprehension Activity: Sequencing

Directions: Good readers know that following the *sequence of events* is important to understanding the text. Fill in what comes next in the food chain of this poem.

_____

_____

_____

◯   **Flowers**

Write at least three sentences telling what this poem is all about. Is a food chain necessary? Why? Don't forget beginning capitals and ending punctuation.

1. _____

_____

2. _____

_____

3. _____

_____

Said the Spider

(SPIDER)	(NARRATOR)	(FLY)
"I won't hurt you,"		
	said the spider.	
"I'm a carnivore."		
		"A fancy word,"
	the fly replied.	
		"I've not heard that before."
"We'll look it up,"		
	the spider said.	
"Come use my dictionary."		
	By the time the fly was wise, was he sorry?	
		"Very!"

© 2009 *Partner Poems for Building Fluency*   Scholastic Professional

Said the Spider

Comprehension Activity: Making Inferences

Directions: Sometimes writers state information directly in the text; other times, readers must infer information from details in the text. Decide whether the following statements are true or false, and then think about how you knew. Did the poet say so in the poem, or did you use a detail from the poem to infer?

The spider told the fly he would not hurt him.   True or False

How do you know?_____

The spider was trying to trick the fly.   True or False

How do you know?_____

The food web keeps nature in balance.   True or False

How do you know?_____

Spiders are more intelligent than flies.   True or False

How do you know?_____

The fly was prey.   True or False

How do you know?_____

The fly was very sorry in the end.   True or False

How do you know?_____

Spiders eat meat.   True or False

How do you know?_____

The spider shared his dictionary with the fly.   True or False

How do you know?_____

Night Crossing

1ST ANIMAL)	(2ND ANIMAL)	(TRUCK)
		ZZROOOM!
Come on! Let's cross!		
	No. **Not yet.**	
We can make it.		
	No. **We can't.**	
		ZZROOOM!
Okay. Now.		
	No. **Not yet.**	
We can make it.		
	No. **We can't.**	
		ZZROOOM! *ZZROOOM!*
Wait?		
	Wait.	
Now?		
	Wait.	
Now?		
	Now!	
Run!	**Run!**	

Night Crossing

Comprehension Activity: Making Predictions

Directions: Good readers *predict* what will happen next in the story. What do you think will happen next in this story? Write your prediction and why you chose it. Compare your prediction to your classmates' predictions. Are they different but still logical?

Prediction:

_____

_____

_____

_____

Why I made this prediction:

_____

_____

_____

_____

Write a story or poem based on your prediction.

Use the back of this sheet or a separate piece of paper.

Passing in the Night

(MOUSETRAP)

Mousey, Mousey,
Come here, please.

It's all for you,
My little treat.

Step right up
And take a bite.

A tasty way
To end it too.

(MOUSE)

**Mmmm, cheese!
Cheesy cheese!**

**Oh! I want
Your cheese to eat!**

**A tasty way
To start the night!**

**No thanks, I'll leave
Your cheese for you.**

Passing in the Night

Comprehension Activity: Making Connections

Directions: Good readers make sense of what they read by *making connections* to information and events they have experienced, observed, or read about. Make a connection by thinking of a time you tried to persuade someone to do something. Write about it. Be ready to share your piece with your classmates.

_____

_____

_____

_____

_____

_____

_____

_____

_____

_____

_____

Like Cats and Dogs

(CAT)	(DOG)
I'm a precious pussy cat.	
	I'm a handsome dog.
Sure you're handsome— Like a bat!	
	You're precious—like a frog!
You bark and bark and bark and bark!	
	You waste the day asleep.
You snore the minute it gets dark.	
	You pussyfoot and creep.
Folks adore my glowing eyes.	
	They love my waggy tail.
My nose is such a perfect size.	
	My nose can smell a trail.
My nose can smell a tiny mouse.	
	My nose can smell a rabbit.
I love to race around the house!	
	I love the racing habit!
I always thought that dogs were rough.	
	I thought that cats were horrible.
We were wrong!	
	'Cause sure enough.
Both of us are adorable.	**Both of us are adorable.**

Like Cats and Dogs

Comprehension Activity: Compare and Contrast—Venn Diagram

Directions: Good readers can *compare and contrast* information in the text. Compare and contrast cats and dogs and then write a paragraph describing which would make a better pet.

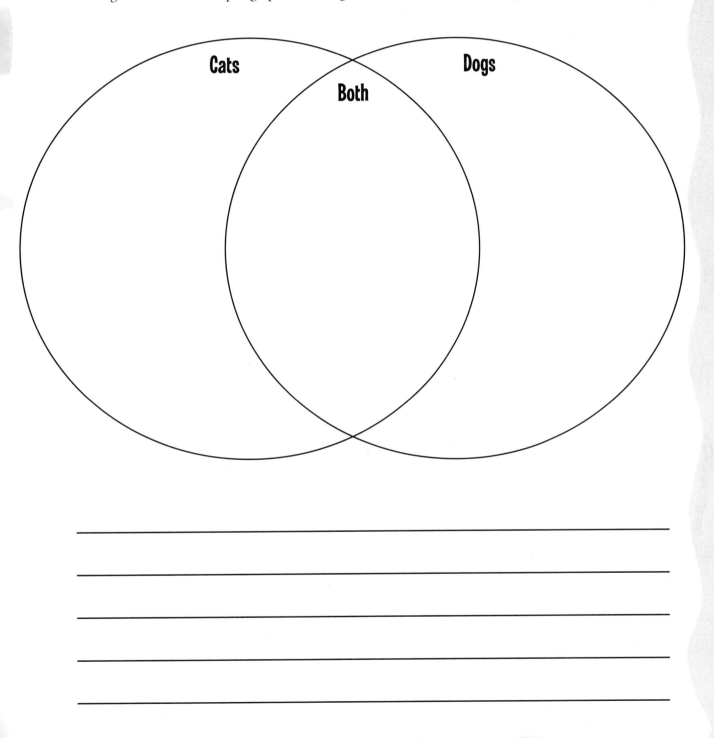

_____

_____

_____

_____

Road Signs

(1ST VOICE)	(2ND VOICE)	(3RD VOICE)	(4TH VOICE)
Sleep here! My rooms are great!			
	My used cars are all first rate!		
		My ice cream is smooth as silk!	
			My cows give the freshest milk!
Turn left!			
	Turn right!		
		Speed up!	
			Slow down!
My restrooms are the best in town!			
	We will tell you what to do!		
		We will tell you where to go!	
			Trust us! Signs know everything
You'll			
	ever		
		need	
			to know!

92   © 2009 *Partner Poems for Building Fluency* Scholastic Professional

Road Signs

Comprehension Activity: Making Connections

Directions: Good readers make sense of what they read by *making connections* to information and events they have experienced, observed, or read about. Make connections to the poem "Road Signs" by creating signs that advertise your school, your home, and something you are fond of.

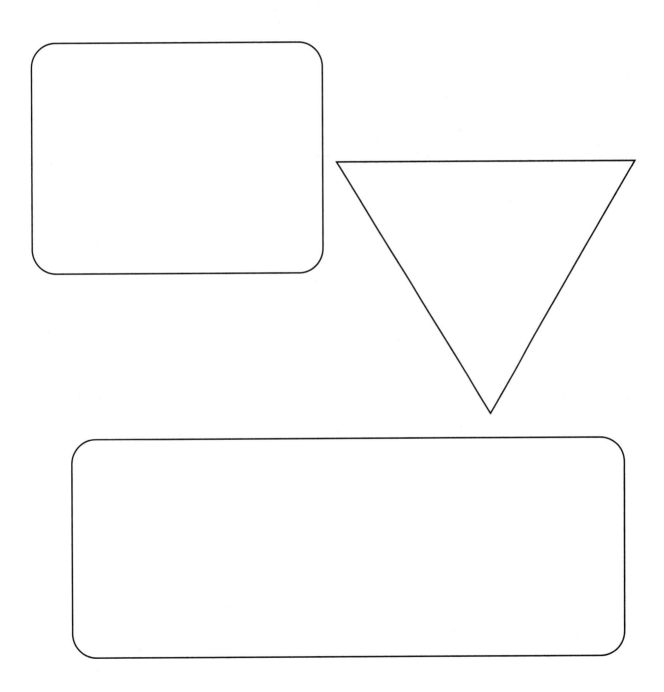

I Did Worse

(1ST VOICE)   **(2ND VOICE)**   **(3RD VOICE)**   **(4TH VOICE)**

Once I swallowed
A greasy gnat.
What's worse
Than that?

Once I swallowed
A slimy fly.
I thought
I'd die.

I swallowed a slug
Inside a waffle.
It was awful!

I finished my spinach
With a happy grin.

Yuck!   **Yuck!**   *Yuck!*
You win!   **You win!**   *You win!*

© 2009 *Partner Poems for Building Fluency*   Scholastic Professional

I Did Worse

Comprehension Activity: Making Connections

Directions: Good readers make sense of what they read by making connections to information and events they have experienced, observed, or read about. Write about connections you can make to the characters in this poem. Use your connections to write your own poem.

Describe something a brother, sister, or friend did that was gross.

_____

_____

_____

Describe something you did that was worse.

_____

_____

_____

Describe something else a brother, sister, or friend did that was gross.

_____

_____

_____

Who was the winner?

_____

_____

References

Irwin, J. W. (1991). *Teaching reading comprehension processes* (2nd ed.). Boston: Allyn & Bacon.

National Reading Panel. (2000). Report of the National Reading Panel: Teaching children to read. Report of the subgroups. Washington, DC: U.S. Department of Health and Human Services, National Institutes of Health.

Rasinski, T. V. (2003). *The Fluent Reader.* New York: Scholastic.

Rasinski, T. V., & Hoffman, J. V. (2003). Theory and research into practice: Oral reading in the school literacy curriculum. *Reading Research Quarterly, 38,* 510–522.

Rasinski, T. V., Padak, N. D., Linek, W. L., & Sturtevant, E. (1994). Effects of fluency development on urban second-grade readers. *Journal of Educational Research, 87,* 158–165.

Rasinski, T., & Stevenson, B. (2005). The effects of Fast Start reading, A fluency based home involvement reading program, on the reading achievement of beginning readers. *Reading Psychology: An International Quarterly, 26,* 109–125.

Samuels, S. J. (1979). The method of repeated readings. *The Reading Teacher, 32,* 403–408.

Stahl, S., & Heubach, K. (2005). Fluency-oriented reading instruction. *Journal of Literacy Research, 37,* 25–60.

Tompkins, G. E. (2007). *Literacy for the 21st century: A balanced approach.* Columbus, OH: Pearson.

Wilfong, L. (2008). Building fluency, word-recognition ability, and confidence in struggling readers: The Poetry Academy. *The Reading Teacher, 62,* 4–13.